DIGSITE

DIGSITE

OWAIN NICHOLSON

NIGHTWOOD EDITIONS

2016

Nightwood Editions
P.O. Box 1779
Gibsons, BC VON 1VO
Canada
www.nightwoodeditions.com

COVER DESIGN: Topshelf Creative, Gibsons, BC
TYPOGRAPHY: Carleton Wilson

Canada

Canada Council   Conseil des Arts   BRITISH COLUMBIA
for the Arts   du Canada   ARTS COUNCIL
                                            An agency of the Province of British Columbia

Nightwood Editions acknowledges financial support from
the Government of Canada through the Canada Book Fund and
the Canada Council for the Arts, and from the Province of British
Columbia through the British Columbia Arts Council and the Book
Publisher's Tax Credit.

This book has been produced on 100% post-consumer recycled,
ancient-forest-free paper, processed chlorine-free
and printed with vegetable-based dyes.

Printed and bound in Canada.

CIP data available from Library and Archives Canada.

ISBN 978-0-88971-324-6

To my grandparents and my mentors;
who believe and inspire.

CONTENTS

I.

Diggin' in the Rain   11
Arrival   12
Atlas Excavates   14
HhOw 53   15
Dawn Tree Climb, Whiteshell   16
3.7 Million Years   18
Catechism   21
Kid Grendel on Summer Vacation   24
Manitoba Solstice   26
Without Treatise   28
Omens   29
Taphonomy   30
Celebration   31
Into Adulthood   34

II.

The Water's Cycle   37
Chickadees in the Winter   38
Sisyphus Takes Atlas on a Hike   39
Natural Selection   40
Under the Lungs of the Sun   42
Let Us Dismember "Cultural Superiority"   48
The Loyalist's Cycle   50
Sacrilege is an Artifact   52
The Coward's Cycle   53
For a Moment, Consider Panic   54

III.

Moth-Hour Falling   57
All the Others   58
Stasis   60
Tracks in the Coulee   62
Hypocrisy Beneath the Sun   64
Ethnocide   66
Apostasy   68
Hunter   71
Insert [Creed] Here   72
The Half-Sleeping   74
Last Test   76
Day [number?]   78

IV.

Silkie   81
The Pompeii Premise   82
Peregrinations   84
Principle of Faunal Succession   86
Principle of Superposition   88
Survival   90
Blastocyst   91
Love, at Distance   92
Reparation   93
Digsite   94
The Silent Spruce   100

Acknowledgements   101
About the Author   103

I.

How you understand the dispossessed now,
in the bush so long there is no expedition
from perdition except calls home.
Your phone is static detachment from the voice you need,
cutting in and out. Their face lays pictured next to you
each empty sleep in the long, bright nights.
Distance is a mantra, and it says, *This is not everything.*
But you are here, and this is not your room.

ATLAS EXCAVATES

There is no place like the past. Tomorrow
he will dig where bones were laid.
Where lives made lives, made lives bear

the raspberry heat-puckered hearth.
He will dig the colours as they change.
He will lay the shovel across thin scapulae
and at his feet, each season is action-turned-
consequence, the barren stratigraphy.

He will clone pre-history from a still, breathless rib.

There is nothing for us but the assembly line
of our own skeletons: contiguous spine, transverse
inferior skull-moon, atlas-and-axis, descending crescents,
wane-and-wax; every ancestral genera

lowing deep in the pelvis. This gibbous past
where no remnants are found.
His back bends to the bones,
bare and bare and bare.

HhOw 53

There were people here. Maybe 8–9 kya,
by stratigraphy. Perhaps, barely post-glacial.

The sun makes neck, shoulders, and occiput a hearth.
Red as soil heat-treated, orange, raspberry-shaped.

No tools: only cores, core frags, flakes.
One Beaver River Sandstone point yesterday –
the ugly arrowhead rounded at the apex; inferior prongs
knobbed like dog toes (all points are beautiful to archaeologists).
Shifting 9 m² between us today; each unit down 60 cm
(50 cm in bare levels). 1 and ¹/₂ units each.

We haven't found a hearth. It gnaws, that absence.
60 cm exhumed in these two blocks.
40 dredged before lunch – only 20 yesterday,
grubbing around roots thicker
than the mouths of poacher's traps.
A hearth means people stayed.

No tools still – there is no stillness here – only the point.
The no-hearth site a people's threadbare memory
of transition and heat-stroke again, full-sleeved
as we are, laughing too much at anything.

Sometimes we wonder why we dig.
The laughter dies away, always, and sun – a squatter.
We aren't six feet down, but you could bury someone this deep.

DAWN TREE CLIMB, WHITESHELL

Worried arms; blistered hands.
Pine sap caulked to raw skin;
sheer height a boreal call.
Nails ratchet into bark and bough.
Mist rucks from the creased lake,

    scabs earth to air.
Prickled by needles you walk a limb.
The branch above roughens palms
and, between these bent arms, you hang.
Grasp at the wisdom gods earned
for their dying. But you don't have time
for resurrection, only a canoe ride
and the day's coming heat.
Maybe you can catch a pike for dinner.

To the north, bedrock bulges the mist.
The old stone humped and hunkered
beneath two pines curled out and bowed.
That wind-gnawed ridge a bison skull.
You want to climb that hill too, stand
tiny on the frontal plate, and listen
to the skirls of water that slap the base,

the sunken mandible. Chilled limbs have forgotten
the pump of blood. You can't remember
     descent. It's not hard,
hang and clutch and balance and hang again.
You have no runes or wisdom to bring to breakfast,
only your grubby self to blow
at campfire embers and fetch water.

You would tell your parents how to climb.
The sting of cuts opened as you brachiate
and mount each rung. You would tell
them of each mythos you've climbed –
every tree a world. You would tell
them about the palate of that savage freedom,
the cold air above earth. You would tell
them about the caul of the wild,
but you can't articulate the roots of it.

3.7 MILLION YEARS

Storms dignify across your back –
a boat, a shell, a gourd; an acacia's genome
mythologizing at the coils of this world.

Lucy, darling, you walk on two legs.
How do you understand the typhoon's
cacophony from your mouth? It's unseemly.

The excavation is a catacomb
and each esoteric malady
is sweat on your brow
and the parasites in your intestines.
The remedies you are entrusted
into follow the letters another trusts.
What has come, the earth tells you,
has come and come and come.

Lucy, honey, at least try not to walk like a cock-out male.
Predators will stalk the slash of your figure above the plain,
your tall shade saturating sky in the eyes of hunters.

You squat by the pit
like half a brain-case,
little evolutions lost
in the descending clay
eras, ready for in situ
assembly before any diatribe
about how one may have lived.

You sharpen the shovel,
and lean into it because this work,
righteous or not, you think,
has prepared you for the old darkness –

Lucy, darling, how ugly the curves of your hips when upright.
How will daughters ever cling to you?
Why must you insist on peeling sticks for termites,
breaking with your teeth their crunchy bodies?

– what untenable years you stood upon,
stand in, will excavate?
The earth's horizons, troweled bright,
ladder you deep into epochs that deny
your focused dates, so much in association,
so much your data must isolate.

How are you so strong, my daughter,
having scavenged brains/bivalves/serpents in the acacia
beneath the lungs of the sun?

And you can't deny
the vulgar light of your own culture –
why will none walk frankly
just to share or know another
like the blush of berries?
All you've managed
is scavenged, tessellated fossils;
your body has forgotten
its own history of being strong.

Ash falls, lightless, lighter than rain.
Lucy, honey, how do you carry your daughter
upon your hip, always that suck upon your breast;
always only two prints behind and two ahead?

And you can't deny
the impermanence of your
culture, this rain a blessed
jurisdiction keeping sun
from the burnt-hearth-clay-mosaic
across your back. Storms
story down shoulders,
down belly, across
the uterus you bear,
full or empty,
by your vast acacia bones.
Each must trust their skeleton –

Lucy, daughter, what as made you able to walk
from this pestilence, and bear your daughters
into all displendent strata?

CATECHISM

0–10 cm
You know this darkness, *don't you?* –
a bezoar in the cartilaginous caverns
of your geology. Vesicles mountain close to your surface,
hearth-red from the sun. The vast glacier sky:
no crevasses to shelter your solar-tongued skin.

10–20 cm
Mossies smeared dead
in your ear – a line of sap
or bitumen that crudes
buccal gorge, gullet, lungs –
having eaten into you before dying.

And your lips are blackfly fat and tongue
and eyelids are numbed, subsuming DEET-slick sweat.
The earth comes out before the crude harvest.
Is there any water left to subdue the stones,
kicking thunder in your belly?

20–30 cm
So much is missing.
Centimetres ground out by your boots:
thromboses erecting wattle-and-daub huts
on the banks of your wet-season
arterial riverbanks – post-holes in the clay;
fire-stains like a withered placenta;
petrified wood blade from some first burning
cooled a hundred-million years in bog,
water drained by glaciers and tools struck

from fossilized, heart-line matrix.

30–40 cm
Digging will recommence after
this paid, fifteen-minute break:
what you wouldn't sacrifice
for a breeze; what you wouldn't put to the shovel
by the weight of your body
for a cool meniscus to rip into nude
and bathe peeling skin like your ancestors,
nakedly in their graves.
What fucking moron declared
your nativity disgraceful?

40–50 cm
All things in situ
where something exterminated them.

50–60 cm
Dust has entered your many returns.
There's only so much one may be, made from mud,
and all you need is a piss
but the climb out of the unit is already monumental
with what's dug out.
Like the last dehydrated purge,
it'll only tell you what you already know –
    Boneless
    Casteless
– and you're already beneath all cultural layers.

60–70 cm
Of course, this is all a matter of point-of-view,

and the living floor can't tell you where earlier people walked.
How you wish your trowel would score out
more than differing natural sediment
that the millennia laid down,

maybe something important like long-bone, skull, biface
but the bugs are out and there's no shade.
In the stratigraphy, only the overwhelming singularity:
someone having run towards the sun
and someone, later, against it.

70–80 cm
Heatstroke comes without irony,
but what does it matter?
And there is nothing else but to vomit;
your geological body excavated, wetly,
abandoned by your own hand.

80–90 cm
There is no way to remain
but in effigy. Caulk yourself
in mud and renewal shall not touch
nor denounce
your nakedness.

90–100 cm
And what is left but to burn it all down?
The next creed will whelp in your strata
and curse your *derogatory* horizon,
digging thinly for something
which must have had more meaning.

KID GRENDEL ON SUMMER VACATION

So much ash in the sky from the week's slash-burning
that the days are an imposition. Across the lake,
the blackened forest is askew as if giants had hiked the mountain
and hammered each sapling in one-by-bloody-one.

The boy is no giant: bronze body almost mummified by the sun.
He may never be a man (it's hard to know) and what, even,
does that mean? Maybe just a boy who hasn't tasted another
and is taught that this is a shame he must rectify;
    a slingshot boy who breaks every faceted image
    of himself in bottles cast from the porch
    before night loses gravity and disperses.

He's just tall enough to have his bones shunted into the earth,
flesh cremated like the forest and tilled into field to fertilize
something useful: peppers, flax, the hemispheres of apples
grown slipknotted. What little he is,
burnt away like a comet hauled into the *sun.*

Every morning he attends school, regurgitating
mostly irrelevant skills while sitting in the desks
where they carve names, curses, the stories
they should not know about each other
(because they do not realize how simply persecution begins).
Perhaps he will reforest the clear cuts
where giants plant saplings as if each tree were a skeleton,
fractured by the expectations their forebears
knot into their upbringing like stones to a body
and the body cast into the lake.

Everyone needs gravity, the kid knows,
some small arson to cleanse all the bullshit
he is told as if he won't understand,
won't listen in the lurk
at the top of the stairs,
won't hide his passage
by mapping each floorboard creek;

as if he won't evolve from his own monstrosity.

MANITOBA SOLSTICE

December 21, 2010

I

My cousins and I crowd the fire –
a powwow of three. The old hearth
yellow-and-grey slate rippled like cooled
lava. In the basement, blankets robed
about our shoulders, we clamp cocoa
in our laps. Scald tongues to pool
that hot in our bellies. Heat swathes us –
we smile, drinking the orange-damp dark.

II

Grandma moved north of Brandon.
Here, our parents evict us: "Play outside,"
they say. "You'll thank us some day."
Lost among hills of winter and birch,
we prowl this toboggan Sahara. We watch
a bobcat broad-pawed in the snow
until we shiver blue-lipped and cold.
We jitter inside to thaw. Bobcat startles
into brush. Cocoa waits to burn palms.

III

Now, our little cousins hunch before the new
glass hearth, soot-tinted. Cocoa mugs unsteady
in sled-chilled hands. When Auntie hustles
them to bed we circle the stone, lay
another husk of birch on embers like eyes
in ashen lids. Alone, we drink from the necks
of green bottles and look for thirty-ones,
fifteens and muggins. Before the flames,
we speak in nods and shrugs and carry this night
on awkward shoulders for the first time.

WITHOUT TREATISE

12 cm
  down

a worm tastes blind muzzle across distal phalanges
(pisiform, trapezium, lunate) and your first thought,
only a couple metres above muskeg, is:
    Eat the gifts of the earth;
    hunger is war without treatise.

It could be a gambit with Pythagoras
all over again (the worm coils
through fingers, which should be gloved
but it's just too much,
innumerable safety protocols and all;
and the point of an arts degree,
you postulate, was to get away
from the stuff "never to be used" wasn't it?)

    A-squared [work-energy-deficit]
    multiplied by B-squared
    [energy-sum-of-worm]
    – some 9 inches –
    equals C-squared
    [net-energy-renewed-
    by-the-hypotenuse-of-a-worm]

Crew lead interrupts, says,
"Hey, you look dehydrated."

OMENS

Lightning. All the day's heat parched the earth. We drove home
through the browned stalks of rushes; my tanning hide stretches

beneath the sun. I cannot wring water from my hair, fearing
the helix will prove false or speak of an old people so homozygous

we could hate them, too. Rain like lithics (chert, quartzite,
flint; a scraper, a blade); bipedality preceded encephalization

and the first copper ingot falls heavy as moose hooves;
bronze and iron, the age after steel, and my shovel moans,

bucked through roots thick as a six-year-old's thigh –
bearing the earth on its mechanical grace. There is rain.

Sometimes I think, there is meaning in people. All night,
thunder, the clash of two rocks underwater. I am often wrong.

TAPHONOMY

Rain warms your body, like the touch of your loved one
at night when your body turns – skin-to-skin, water-
to-water. The rhythmic course upon you is a heart;
each movement is tiny and necessarily impressive.
Body-to-body, until rhythm is singular primary echo.

(Amongst all this vast and meaningless crap)
turn your body to theirs, earth-to-earth;
rock-and-stone compress against the great distances,
faults/oceans/spinning iron core.

Water courses across your skin-to-skin
    like a real sacrifice.

In the wake of your delivery you will be refuted,
    only the image of your burial will take your place.

CELEBRATION

For Lydia and Jacques

"It's time," my father says, "he had a magnificent run."

In my basement suite, pale light through the pale blinds
for the passing of an age. The snow melts in the park
behind the house, what remains of the old river valley
runs in slopes to the river; and before the window,
the dark vibrancy of a planted spruce that, at night,
the streetlamps orange with a vitality not dissimilar
to the burning of a bush or halo – I will be able to pilgrim
this journey, for celebration (in memoriam).

When I was little (maybe three):
we fence with Christmas-wrapping cardboard tubes
until the knightly graces of our weapons
accept too much brutality and, forced to treaty,
we disarticulate the illusion. With no choice
but peace, he leads me to the pool where I learn
buoyancy with the aid of secondary wings.
I throw toys into the deep and watch him dive –
the white of his hair a light like a crown.
For complicity in the drowning of my toys,
I am arrested in the living room, naked after the swim.
Let alone for just too long I may no longer help
but squat and pee between arctic chairs,
before a canvas-mounted polar bear exploring
the scents of some unfamiliar and engaging green world.
He returns to me as I finish. He sighs, says nothing
to grandchild three, and proceeds to clean.
I stand by and hold my penis in a triage of shame

31

and absent disinterest in the utilitarian means of my relief,
anxiously decided that cleanliness is for a time after
playing the next, and the next, game.

When I was ten (or so):
Grandma's feet on the Audi dash, the window down
and her toes are the crooked and flush stalks of grains
on every horizon that surrounds passage to the mountains.
I toy with a camera, take pictures, know no better
and open it road-side, in the sun, my curiosity too great.
We stop at a diner where the pancakes are too much
(except there's never enough syrup), and Grandpère turns
my unfocused disappointment for the blind photographs
to his hands, raised above the meal: "Opening the abdomen,"
he explains, "right side above pelvic crest, reach inside,
don't pull. See with your hands."
(For blindness need not be a curse,
and loss is not always what it seems.)
He removes the bloated primordial organ. "Scalpel, please,"
he says. Across the linoleum table, I pass a scalpel,
tangible only by the imagination we offer each other.
"Leave enough to tie the intestine closed," he says;
what follows is knotting the body against itself to heal.

When I was seventeen (and graduated into adulthood):
we gather for drinky-poos and chat. Dinner and dance
and all manner of evening stuff would follow;
but, at some point, we walk to the water, unhurried.
The strand of trees along the lake, full and leafing,
and June blossoms. Worn-dark gradients path among ferns
to uneven stone beach a-kiss with slow slotting water
learning its last distance without cessation (rising, always,
for a further stone, some distant shore). A moment together.
The mountains cascade endlessly and counteract
the infinite, rotating deep. Quiet and reposed,
an instinct in me to witness, silently,
the nave of the valley and redact my day-to-day
the way Grandma replaced the film roll-by-roll –
always focusing perception through unblinded apertures
at what may be described as fire: to warm each other;
and, after, to preserve life in ember as our ancestors learned
to resurrect light, and bear our burning forward.

INTO ADULTHOOD

The bedrock is cool against their soles.
Close-tucked mist drifts through the woods
like white blood cells.
They eat from mugs speckled blue like sparrow eggs.
      Yesterday was too cold to swim but today,
this morning, it will be colder. They chew
instant meal: dried apple, powdered syrup,
oats soft as weevils.
      They walk determined into the lake, until
the water hits pubis. The mist deepens,
as if they swim the bedrock above the meniscus.
Now, there is only the controlled
flagellation of limbs. From beneath, a
soul is fog. Here there is no world.

II.

THE WATER'S CYCLE

The rain unends, little bee,
and my boat compasses on the water.

There's a pike on the line
and I don't know about the hook
but the world is scuttled.

Clay never leaves skin unmarked;
the good work bevelled my joints
but the earth was empty.

The pike rudders against fin-skin waves
but keel, hull and gunnel
are only substructure.

The heart suffers
because that's what we earn –

    Always how we sleep:
    a skeleton grinning
    into the last skeleton's
    degenerate skull in the burial pit;
    what would you say
    if that were you, constructing
    who you thought I was,
    interpreting down to me?

– I think we carry living too long.

CHICKADEES IN THE WINTER

In the barren hedges, though early, chickadees vocalize
whatever it is they disseminate as important.

Imagine, their wings give solidity to this reality; in the churning
that recedes, their hunt decries precedent to exist.

The world twists us, as if we plummet and plummet
and cannot fly. But this is not your quo or que.

When you wake, do not startle to find your arms are feathered.
Spot those thermals you could take and don't.

Your wings carry you through this world. Hunt.

SISYPHUS TAKES ATLAS ON A HIKE

Slope-and-gravel switchbacks ascend from parking,
meagre merge ramps, highways. Alpine fields stretch before you
(but never take wilderness for freedom). Against bare feet,
little yellow-and-purple flowers dip like bees tasting for pollen.
Walk until you come to a small lake.

    Undress without rush because there is no one to call "fool"
    (except you can always find someone) –

and none may declaim your form or disarticulate your aesthetics
and faiths (but isn't there always some other demand upon you?)
like bobguys jackhammering concrete for the newer infrastructure.

Nudely into the crisp, until sun is dream upon skin.
Underwater your soul is an X-ray in sun. Don't forget,
the lake is only a lens. Ripples you may not help but commit
tiger you; this time there is neither hammer nor chain and, yet,
    somehow, you find yourself drowning –
    camouflaged by your own design.

NATURAL SELECTION

The mangoes are fresh. Thick-cut wedges.
Juice runs all the way to elbows.

Sun surf. Waves photograph at peak.
Crash.
The mango offs in the water
as you paddle tummy down

into azure glass where dark shapes tail.
Wait for swell, legs dangled in cool-warm brine.

At the end of the rush, the city;
sunlit stalagmites scrape sky –
before now: brick and concrete,
cedar, postholes, middens –
and the beach is sand paint swipe
meeting mixed green forest-wedge
until highway, evolving beyond what
may once have been animalia.

And this is yours, not the road
which may not be inherited only salvaged,
but running, running, running.

Swell tempo felt, the ebb on your cilia.
You forward paddle, shoulders lift-and-set.
Lift-and-set.

You are horses at gallop on the tan-grass hills
that selected running until running was perfected.

The wave lifts. Carries as the line of your mare's spine,
all vertebrae in place –

hurtling into crush, against all gravity.
Salt spray on your cheeks.

All the photographs tumble like caverns
where ancestors begat and left jagged mandibles.

You mare at the apex of the herd, the stocks of ancient grains
parted and spraying the hillocks like stars on the clearest nights,

and find purchase. On the shore, the city never fostered belonging.

All that matters is running until waves plain and you collapse
into shoal, shaking-and-shaken, waiting to run again.

UNDER THE LUNGS OF THE SUN

June 8

At some point, hard-hammer night eraillures
into shim morning. We kick shovels from present
through approx. 30 cm of the last ten thousand years.
Give or take a few decades. The glaciers reopened.
Stale silt-smell, musk…
can you hear the breathing earth?…
could be the muskeg, could be my steel-toes.
Same difference, really.

I sit back on my haunches, flex wrists and elbows
which are all crooks and splints from jarring shovel and trowel
against ironstone. At 26.6 cm, a BRS blade. Our work cubes
the land with 10-cm arbitraries. My hands bleed.
Glove-rubbed blisters erode palms, growing like glaciers
on the move. Skin and pus burgeons without cessation.
Tonight, I will knife the pockets between fingers, lifelines,
some strange hubris above my pisiform.

Ravens, big fuckers, steal at our gear; but it's too heavy,
the soul within, the food, the perceived necessities.
The sun lungs down on us, our breath uncatchable,
reaping scorched necks like a kestrel dismembering beetle,
frog, pine marten. Every living is a kind of sacrifice,
and each burial a monument for the beaks of scavengers.

July 8

When did good work become a moose, driven for days
before snapping wolves? The retreat of glaciers our past,
just another butchery: sold, minted into coins that melt
and melt away like sweat on some fat bastard who sits
in his truck, idles the engine for A/C and satellite radio:
he watches the rise-and-fall of neck-to-sole Nomex coveralls;
fails to empathize from whence he scavenged
and complains about the difficulties of his 21 days
(in this economy) to a wife who raises children
against the 60, 75, 90 k ejaculated into his truck.

We hike passed, follow the old river valleys. We want the west;
if I look across, a boy has risen five thousand years ago
into sun. He stirs embers awake against the eventual
arthritis in his knuckles and wrists from pressing antler
into stone so he may hunt with his father, with his son
but that's a different lease. We dig burnless, in the eastern darkness
where the bugs are known to swarm the lungs of moose
until they drown in their own blood.

Who are we to determine your remains expunged
by the acidic soil? All the voices, around all the hearths
(we will, thankfully, never record so many souls make us
witness our own) preying at the long-zero horizon: slogging
through this chest-deep frigid bog; this sun on our shoulders
like standing near enough to fire that your own juices
dribble down your skin: this living a sin condensing
like dew into the morrow because it's all an assimilation,
all a migration, all a hopelessness we share.

We offer what water we have
(when that's gone, pack up and move on).

August 8

Rosehips thorn my knees. I'll need to knife 'em
in the shower tonight, so heat eases skin against blade.
We follow slope down into coulee. Crew lead says,
"Shit. There's a den." Look: where she kneels
and leans into the earth, a hare or marten's torn body
writhes but that's just flies and larvae and ants…
"Let's back up. Follow the high ground around."
We turn and scramble atop the coulee.
Someone checks the GPS and those who followed now lead:
another 867 metres.

Someone could break their leg in this deadfall.

"So a few seasons back," says crew lead, "we're outta cell service
for a few hours after checking in and all's good but the sat-phone
won't connect and it's hot as fuck. We get to the argos
and the phone goes fucking crazy. The safety crew.
They're about to fire up the 'copter for us. Turns out,
one of the camp heads went assessing cut-lines
and slipped on some chainsaw scrub. Anyway,
this little sapling trunk ripped right through his femoral artery.
So, watch your going; we're a click outta service if you try dying."

September 8

A pine marten drags a wood frog into her barrow,
kicking. It is a good day for scavengers like us… except,

there are none like us… finally, my shovel breaks against
the whatever-millionth root but my hands are wood.
By mid-morning our digging falters and our skin is raw
with sunstroke and our lungs feel like someone else's
ragged breathing, and this is a ball-and-chain
moorin' to Earth and we've lost our ragg'd bearing…

If we were buried, would this alienated breathing
have mattered? [*Laughter*]
What tracks but graves does anyone leave?

The digging empties. There is little water left.
All our worker's souls could be purchased like lotto tickets.
In the heat, the breathing of a truck-struck coyote
where we left our trailers. The empress of rushes lived
during the abscessed sun's grinding tutelage,
and now some thinly subsistence finds her.
I would wriggle into her body like a haematophage;
because this is progress's dying, gum-slid bitch-tongue:
our blunt-browed skull beating, each pace
refusing acknowledgement, the furlongs undocumented.
What if our species' cairns are like ticks twisted off
and festering in someone else's anagenesis?

October 12

We watch a bear watch our trucks come to a halt.
She has chewed through her own leg.
She watches us from her haunches. We turn the engines off.
Wait. Three cubs run into the alder and spruce.
We take out our maps, radio that poachers have traps out here,
and consider sat images. We chose three moraines to hit,

and drive slow, so *the bears know we've left.*
Inevitably, another engine will grind the gravel back this way;
maybe to poach her cubs, maybe to poach her cubs' cubs.
Maybe there won't be bears, just the mine.

Returned to camp, we crunch inside and untie our muskeg-
soaked boots.It's hot enough for what little water our bodies
retain to sweat through our natural-fibre trousers
because synthetics melt if there's a fire, so we've been told.
The twelve-by-ten room is enough for bed,
dresser, static-brushed TV. I rinse the dirt off for dinner;
my bloodless palms could strike sparks. Beneath the nails,
in the creases, in the scrapes, around the thorns.
In ruptured blisters dirt floodplains. Will not wash away.
Will not wash away. Language could burn it all down.
Instead, there is quiet in the absence of digging,
the furlongs of opened earth refilled and tomorrow stretches
into the boreal forest the way our DNA is a spine, a ridge cut
into by the burgeoning and retreating glaciers.How they
come and go. How we dig into our own and find nothing,
and move a few metres along and cut into our own nothing,
and how we move a few metres, drink, sweat, cut into.
Once we followed the animals and praised them.
Now we think ourselves beyond the hunt; and, we are.
I go to bed, my eyes sparking, blinded all day by sun.

October 26

Morning snow slants down like last month's late lightning.
A lasting umber. Dawn rises like moths. Quick snap by raven beak
and the moths disperse, eaten. We have so little time.
Cinnamon on the tree line. Even so late in the season

we will sweat into the afternoon, and then shiver
in the tree shade and the long argo ride back.
Frost when we leave; frost when we return. There are no paths
untravelled. Sometimes when we hike I hear other steps:
perhaps it is the hunting boy with his father,
perhaps it is my own breaking feet
and the sunstroke, ten-thousand-year animal runs,
rosehips and bear shit, kestrels hidden in the sun to hover
and pick the insects off our bodies when we collapse.

I shrug my body back and forth, bent as if I wash potatoes
in a basin in the yard, or how it was to gut pike
on Whiteshell bedrock, and the screen slices dirt in sandy sprays
that waver back and forth, mirages, and by this displacement
reveals the glassy-wire-scratch of quartzite. A slice
like a cornea, a piece of chalcedony.
Crew lead finds three scales of obsidian, greenish
in the evening sun like the reeds and muskeg paths
where we've lost ourselves. How will we emerge from this land?

I read poetry at dinner. The rough men leave me alone.
They and I hear the ribs beneath the earth.
They and I bend against the yoke.
Strike my palms with stone and I shall give you fire.
Tonight I will not sleep.

LET US DISMEMBER "CULTURAL SUPERIORITY"

We dig and joke, talk about the ball game,
about civil war; sometimes we roughneck
through muskeg and traverse flood-full creekbeds.
We talk of significant others. We complain.

They tell us: write, always write

Some newscaster said we must discuss the use
of banned weapons. Speak about responsibility
for countries only known on a grade-school globe.
Need to dissect cultural dismemberment surgically –
doesn't objectivity heal like sutures?

All mythologies break down, together, again

A silence comes to the work: autumn frost slicks
the humble frog; moss torn by rutting moose; no tracks
in the first snows. I will not write conflict or speak
as if I know the internal sunder of persecution.

Little bee, what difference does my grammar make?

Tell me about the stele of ancient powers,
who the great statues were when bent at the plow
or when weaving baskets and how, maybe,
even they failed our constructs and consummations.

May my words never be eroded by another's citation;
it is there that this language will sinister

How permanent must our mythos have seemed,
germinating each dawn; histories and glaciers
melt and renew; velocity in the breast;
and there is no consolation – let us listen
to the dunes that esker these hearts.

Never answer

THE LOYALIST'S CYCLE

Pine marten rustles in cold turf,
digging up blueberries, archaeology, moose heart.
The earth you walk is a pelt you can't see
in the dark. What you miss lopes away
before your passage through the freeze.
    Disappears.

Moonous luminosity off the snow
is the only guide; the southern scalps
of old birch turn mossy faces into the cold.
Your palms cannot find the way north.
For the first time your hands are derelict
(and turning blue, by the feel of it).
Some bald-faced raven will eat
your fingers and regurgitate the nails
you split scratching the dirt in a last
feeble prayer for a few frost-hard
rosary rosehips to devour and warm
your facile body: another few shivers,
another few steps in the white, white birch.

And you hurt yourself with every night
you recall laid next to another
and chose to roll away rather than endure
their heat, or taste the sweat on their nape,
cup a nipple or pelvis only to trace
their geometry and tattoo yourself
with the oils from their skin, their hair,
the soft cartography you didn't know
would give more than simple boarders.

Heat, like everything else, is an impression –
moose on the roadside poached
from a truck cab; tracks in flood
mudded banks; your body on the snow
as its faults and continents are revealed
by thin teeth, and settles
pallidly into luminous snow.
Alone, forgotten: winter reconciles
your bitter, irrelevant account.

SACRILEGE IS AN ARTIFACT

We say nothing, emptied by the square metres we've dug,
laid in what shade there is to find. Thrice daily we break fast
like all the people like us who have seen as we see
   and who doesn't consume as we do?

We are here for work, yes, but old stories utter
mythos still and when we leave there will be no metaphors,
only who will walk across this land we abandoned and dig
   and who doesn't remember as we do?

These lives are bitter nettles beneath the tongue.
Buried beneath our vocalizations is the only pit
we don't know how to excavate
   must we define ourselves
   by what we leave behind?

THE COWARD'S CYCLE

Lately, one will walk down through the city slickened
with mist to the breakwater, to the first shore, to the first border
where the tide tells how far one may go,
but only part of the time. Here this person will discover
a sun-beached walking stick so as to ease fallen arches.
Early in the morning with it they will bludgeon a pariah dead.

Return through the city: past parliament on its mangled redoubt
and the streets of no witness, not for broken feet or the stooped
body of age, and past jurors who have forgotten the weight
of their knouts. By morning, rodents from the streets beneath
the streets will have eaten through so no gas distends the belly
and no blue-and-pink-veined organs burst rotting
onto the first shore where the stark obelisks
of the first bones are rediscovered, silenced, quickly buried;
until an unknown species' fractured marrow-eaten femur
juts above erosion – epiphyses gnawed away
and whole civilizations hived into what trabecular bone
remains above the sand.
        Dig in beaches and this is what you'll find.
In the ocean's asthmatic breath,
walk the water's crude, spinal apophyses:

tomorrow, all manner will pilgrimage your threshold
as if they have earned that rite.
You will keep your home locked and send all away
even as pariahs whine; for they wake, beaten and matted and torn
and are not dead, being devoured from the inside.

FOR A MOMENT, CONSIDER PANIC

How you wake in the night with the sun
unset and the bugs, even inside, never ending
(never enough here for *sapiens*, only use):
for a moment, consider panic.

How you smuggle close to your partner's breathing.
They aren't here, you remember, and then rememory
cupping pelvic crescent just above their sex

but even intimacy only goes so deep, like ice
skinning alien planets; the blue of their atmosphere
so alike to yours, but not quite what you need.

III.

MOTH-HOUR FALLING

Sun pumpkins the swaying aspen.
The forest approaches slumber
and white spruce twirl their penumbra skirts.
Today, wind tore trees in half.
And yes, if a tree falls, we hear it.

Our labours remain behind us, thickly,
and the moth-hour is falling

It's a long day ending, and we bomb through
a cut-line nearly reclaimed by bog and black
spruce and wind-walloped trunks that lie askew
like the limbs of someone loved, who took too seriously.

Are we good? Bats eat moths right out of the night

The sun lows and the moon third-quarter wanes high.
The tracks we leave will freeze. Isn't it always this way?
Two hours overdue, driving tired chassis just far enough,
whether we want the trail or not,
and we forget that we hear the trees.

When were we good as we could be?

Maybe tonight, in the moth-hour,
our bodies won't keep failing.

ALL THE OTHERS

The old neighbourhood is nearly unrecognizable.
Remember the lilacs and honeysuckle?
Those living Great Walls delineating
one community from the next.
Even through the barbs and bark, you played.

Remember four square, tetherball, hide-and-seek?
Games were always ritual, hazing, right-of-passage.
When these hedges bloomed, they bloomed on skin;
shy, until blood left the bruise.

Because it was a boy's world.

Wearing jeans was neither hiding your vagina
nor being ashamed of it. You saved many skirts,
knowing the time and place for delicate lace
and when to bear denim into the rip-and-rip
of bodies earwigging in the brush and bushes
and muddy riverbank: the slow, prairie circulation.

They said girls were thrown in the brown waters,
and never found. How could people be lost in the river –
is it not only so deep?

The bruises never ended.
It was a boy's world, still.

But why would they weep when you pushed
harder than they – playing their own games
meant to humiliate, toughen, crook into Man?

There were girls, in lace,
preserved in the river's clay.
The boys could never understand,
and you pitied them.

Again, you have petitioned the Powers-That-Be
(the pitiful boys in their frigid offices) to study and conserve
this new species, quickly reinvigorating the current.

This spring you walked the river path, the old neighbourhood
nearly recognizable. The lilacs grown
viciously thick. Drowned bruises bloom
behind rapids where current separates over rock:
there are no lace-white justifications that may hide
or disseminate the trespasses wrought against them.

Again, you have been refused your right
to find your own sister, and all the others.

STASIS

Each day he tosses an apple, praying the seeds cloud into rain.
The raven gobs at it before another may, even knowing
it is too much for one alone to choke upon.
He watches the birds fight for those bitter seeds.

On the baked roads home he stops avoiding basking snakes,
the occasional lizard. Kestrels swoop low and carry off the bodies –
so heavy their wings beat hard even to lift briefly into the bushes.

At digsite, his shovel cuts through a frog in the moss
who wouldn't move even under the first pressure
(and damn the beast, right?). He tosses it from the screen,
flicks off the blood, goes about his work.

Two days bucking shovel through roots like the pale bones
of a pike gutted out of water and gasping; lately they arrive;

in the grass, what eating has left him in the meagre shade.
"*Will you bring rain so I may rest?*" he asks.

In unison: "*No.*"

"Not even should the waters cleanse me of myself?"

The raven takes off the tabard of an amphibian –
  "We will not fetter our wings to the land
  and this is what we have chosen."

The frog unwinds snakeskin like a hobble –
  "This is not a gift;
  these are the things you made us."

The kestrel regurgitates the seeds of many apples –
  "These are poison and this is not who we are;
  despite my hunting, my children took
  too much from your palm."

When he goes back to work he cannot bear the waste his body
could not accept, each offering miscarried and composting
thinly in the ground. Even with the next sacrifice, castigation
will not close the furlongs he has travelled across the earth,
scalped open and drowning beneath the rain he seeded.

TRACKS IN THE COULEE

It starts with the early tongue of winter –
how chill the late rains, how hard the morning ground;

then

lately, the self a slave arbouring the groves of your outer body,
even as it is devoured by glaciers retracting,
and seeds are never called into germination;

then

shedding early snows and denning into tree throes. Again
this digging: half-tons and feller-bunchers; steel-weathered
stumps from last decade's economy. Another illegal kill-site
poaching minorities: ears, testicles, tongue, ovaries, brain;

then

all the grottos callous with the cultivation between you;
what remnants these thin carcasses, chewed and rent,

hollowed out by the mastication of winter-coated scavengers;

on your skin, your good work is a rotten hide
and you chew willow rind for the bitter numbness
it brings to the bushwhacking; these rains can't chill
your inner gardens, no longer belonging
to you alone – a heart, a little more centred,
beats wetly against yours.

This hunger doesn't even stop at your bones,
gnaws and gnaws and gnaws.

HYPOCRISY BENEATH THE SUN

Mossies cascade, needle-mouths compassing our pheromones –
sight North Star and crawl iron-turning magnetism, praying
we may escape our own reek. Even the indomitable are eaten
and each coulee takes us from sight. Thorns claim clothes,
rip-stop gear, steel-toes; each embankment is fantasy:
no prophet on the esker, in the aspen, in sight from the 'copter.

There is no revolution that may be bloodless,
only reform or extinction. Ask our ancestors
    walking yet;
        their ghosts tore the land (preparing for us).

There is nothing but hypocrisy beneath the sun.
In darkness, only predation.
How they walked, those earlier people, we walk.
We dig the unravelled empires and religions brick-by-hovel,
wattle-and-daub, adobe, tuff pillars left rotting.
These were their mistakes, even mortared with the old
grandeur. They died calling flippant gods to ignore,
and this was original benediction
    (and, maybe also, exorcism).

They bring each carcass back – moose, rhino, antelope,
mammoth – because brutal needs are enough
to excuse what sustains. Tomorrow, each burial.
Someone will record the next *Homo* skull
in a university lab or church catacomb.

They will trace our cook-pit justifications,
    stone-heated and, eaten, our mistruths
    phytolith to our teeth.
Our progeny will laugh
    at our short, pitiful extirpation.

ETHNOCIDE

A culture today (site age requires excavation).
Perhaps in this 10 cm arbitrary the worker's shovel
will budge up flakes, flint chopper, maybe a foetal femur
from precursors who scavenged across this land.
It was a cartography they understood in ways no degree
or work experience may intimate; but the mother died,
and the infant was buried alive on her breast. A kindness.
The worker lifts his pack because another site will be unveiled
in the sands like rapine, all just an accident, of course
(except the dead didn't ask for it, did they?).
But this is all outside the thesis his research grant may allow.
Even as he examines, cites, bibliographs
another comes and excises and excises

> *and no one may*
> *clarify*
> *what may have.*

What if people were sculpture, no matter the material
(ice-bone-wood-stone?): would they language
their living floors, shitholes and cook-pits
    like scripture across megaliths; and what if sand
were to write erosion across their stillborn cairns?
What if they chiselled genocide into the stone
    by antler and soft-hammer, some disgusting
proto-grammar preserved until their children
presbyter and sculpt the next people by this learning?

He wonders how long it will take his people to write
Chosen for Ethnocide on the boxes these artifacts will fill
once brushed, washed, and discarded in little plastic bags –
like an infant tossed into a river (only analysis would tell
which species). So long since, the river has traversed
a couple kms east and silt, delta, floodplain are cut into fields
and sown. Better yet, keep on diggin' up the free world
(non-benefit-hourly minus debt) –
before shipment to warehouse and the femur
will only be ink-on-spreadsheet,
(cardboard or coffin unmatters to the dead)
ignored until the new polity requires glorification
(even this disservice unmatters to the dead).

What if each new predecessor, like mutants
with lactose-tolerant DNA or the last common
ancestor, walked in exodus forever? What if they
were burdened with the potential we will give
their fossils? What if all that is built may only
be built again (no matter which material),
masoned from bezoars each culture propagates:
each people a concretion carving pictographs
into themselves, so knowledge will
not be lost but fossilized –

what if the next creed arrives, burns it all down,
and, uncaring, sows new crops
into the rich matrix of the ashes of the dead?

APOSTASY

I

He listens for soft breathing. It's all make-work projects
in the suburbs – these last weeks spent laying lithics
to dry while fauna dusts away under the brushes;
even gently going, taphonomy collapses disregardless.
Perhaps he could dive into the soil, crawl stratigraphy
as if the layers of the world were stairs worth climbing.

> *This is what the past is:*
> *another AWOL firmament,*
> *some spare tax our bodies*
> *can't sever properly.*

Few days' survey pitting floodplain until his shovel
doesn't even have distal phalanx leverage:
earth punctured like the sockets of a whitetail
on the causeway, mounted by ravens. Ants tongue
each carcass apart and each centimetre could be
an epoch, all the way back, even before bipedalism.
He walks a while, kicks empty another pit, fills it all in.

> *What does it matter*
> *if all is the same?*

Some days, work is walking like blood-shod soldiers.
How horrifying each step into immortality;
finally given over to grave or sea or pyre, refuged
in the dark hives of his own trabecular bone,
only to wake into what twisted cabals in which the living
recast the reimage of the dead – clay, stone, metal –
regurgitated and reborn by his own screely progeny.

    What aberrants are we to blind
    our own and call it service?

    Please do not pity each Lazarus –
    caulk me with earth
    and I will cleanse you
    so we may walk, unafraid
    together, even beneath
    the atmosphere of this world.

II

Ants subcontract into the bones of a juvenile deer,
the fatty bits: gristle and tendon like some sort of Pollock.
Grass hides everything, even smell, until cut square
and levered clear with a bent-bladed shovel. Nothing,
a cache too young in the stratigraphy. This second day:
twenty pits, twenty-some clicks; water run dry.

This is not everything?

He strides into the top layers of the earth, mottled still
with late hearths turned over by plough-and-combine,
and nests in the living floor of some other people
(an animal knelt to the knife by another's body)
    and there are no more hives to hide idolatry –

    I must tell you:
    I've no more words,
    lost like the small ungulate
    struck at night-fold-ninety.
    Under the limit.
    Flung into a ravine.

    Darkness only rock.

    Small breathing, even now:
    tell me you cannot hear it
    and we may, thinly, walk –

little bee, all I taste is lye, hubris, iron.
We could swim out of this if we chose.

HUNTER

Early autumn and winter, already moving in the roost,
peruses clutches of ravens on the eaves,
trucks, a hare thrown to the shoulder.

In three degree-above-freezing morning we listen to wolves
howl.
An accidental kinship to the yowling from machines
felling the forest. I imagine your confusion

reaching that wild place to find Pale-and-Flannel Man
instead, the spicy caul of sap and muskeg under boots: torn
bog-ground beneath the treads of backhoes, dozers, feller-
bunchers

– imagine you, head low and testing, hackles smooth
and loping now, west-and-west where elk
avoid bear-torn aspen and moose tread
unafraid, their philosophical grace too big
for anything but the lights of a blind semi.

Digging, we stop and think to call back,
shout our instincts; say it wasn't us
it never was us and this soil we've opened
we'll cover again for the next glacial age –
for ten thousand years, your paws swift in the snow.

We hesitate to sound our instincts off the aspen,
to shake the boughs, to lower all language into throat-tone.

INSERT [CREED] HERE

Sun slugs the placid palisade of spruce,
some deep-shelled languor on the belly,
related somewhere passed genus. Lugubrious crabbing
across day; slickened mucosa or deep-layered membrane
inherited from a species unseen in broken strata withdrawn
from the ocean like a dividend put towards laying pipe
or crushing ancient lava bed for a garden never twice sat in
by distant owners who visit properties twice a decade,
who can't sell in the markets they've inflated:
stuck with investments the way
they're stuck with a partner (they think)
they remember having something
worth staying for – despite all breakfasts in bed,
evening massages beneath each other's hands,
and morning sex: it all drains into solitary,
practical things which may as well
be frigid for all it matters.

There is a word for this. Perhaps it doesn't matter
if you call *pride-love-solidarity* aloud because
(being too prevalent) people are too busy
to say *cruel-grief-abandonment as it is.*

Be aware: if human touch occurs, the recoil
may shatter children's toys, windows, passers-by
like a gavel bashing levees on all things passion,
and you cannot remember
how it was to treatise the treaties of
No means No and *Yes is Yes*;
how it may have been
to lay honestly against another.

THE HALF-SLEEPING

Constellations have all tucked in.
Even streetlights have lidded,
faint light warmly through skin.
Each city is a city within itself,
arguing; earth truncheons beneath streets.

He is running. The city has too many rules.

> *You will not find help here, love.*
> *But I have cut apples and tossed them*
> *with cinnamon and cardamom.*
> *Please, anoint your hand, dry as it is.*

She flies, unruled.

If dawn were to arrive before its rite,
the dissolute grid would burn away.
All steel-girder skeletons of the inner city
(built in the image of the builders)
would collapse and the cement would crevice
like winter-split skin.

In the darkness he circles home
'round empty lanes, embryonic architectures
cordoned in bright yellows and oranges.
He passes watchers and denies
feeling that he must explain.

When her plane lands, her inner body still flies.

It is too much, these gridlock paths.
Tonight, may the only navigation be by cilia
brushing other bodies
also running in the dark.

I forgot to squeeze lemons for their juice.
When you arrive, love, I will have left.
Spray the apples with citrus –
they will turn before morning.

LAST TEST

We could arrange ourselves like soldiers.
Maybe two-spare, a red line deeply,
and never see a space or break
or glimpse the formation boundary.

Don't tell me I am wrong.
I've burned too many shallow days.

This morning a coyote, empress of rushes,
smote on the highway. Her blood gritly iced
on snow. Still before the sun-below-zero
horizon, I wanted to climb into her jaw,
crawl the cartilage-ribbed throat,
and den into the left ventricle.

My strengths don't diminish yours.

In this darkness not even sun may bridge fur and skin
or the thick-walled muscles of the heart; here, I'd sleep
the sleep of Atlas were he able to lower the skies
to his knees and cool his sweat-furnaced brow against one
or another prevailing wind. Are the many ages of glaciers
strong enough (for each other can we be enough?)
to bear our dreams, however thin, in the crevasses of our skull?

Is it too much being, our own independence?

But glaciers are calving with each step, brightly into the oceans.
I can do nothing about it. Little bee, is this too your life?
When the formation recuperates and our refugee road
freezes again in the night, we may hold each other, thickly,
seeing with the seeing we relearn by touch.

DAY [NUMBER?]

Cremate me and disperse my ghost where crows
will break acorns and chestnuts on my skull.
I will call, *Welcome, stay upon my brow.*
I will laugh with them and think this alright.

There will be no digsite, no one to annotate
cultural details (deposition, stratigraphy,
three-dimensional provenience)
for you will take me out to a paddock, glade, or pond;
somewhere a moose may tread   pause
smell the bitter chalk of dandelion marrow,
and this will be me, and dip its heavy head –
nosing new paths through blueberries, rosehips, briars.

The crows have not come to the grave – today a saw-fallen aspen
or maybe winter-iced muskeg. I think you chase them off.
Neighbour, without them you cull everything I may say.
    I cannot meet you halfway.

IV.

SILKIE

Three seals on rocken spur.
They bathe and you will not wake in distress:
your feet still cool from ocean;
walking through flowers and grasses
which survive their domestication.
Rise from the earth, because nativity is a wild beauty
and no beauty should be routine.
Your roots need not be stripped white,
axed apart, and fashioned into prosthetics.

And this is the risk: dismembering your own intellect
free from the pogrom and ignore the garden
your roots desperately grapple together.
Wear your new skin and swim out to join the seals.
Despite the shelters you abandoned yourself to,

evolution is a caress you may not choose to deny.

THE POMPEII PREMISE

You want to say *No* – end
traversing the limitless furrows
of these streets.
With ever more regularity
no shade, again, and no rain.
Just forest fire burial pyre,
and the rut.

Feet flatten like nail heads
beaten unsteady. Perhaps you'll evolve
to inure this confinement,
fill it with the cycles of your flesh:
skin grinding concrete
as if you were the woman
who yellows the wallpaper with her body –
until all smells are musk, dust,
something deeper: bodily, urine, chemical.

Don't our skeletons
keep the walls from tumbling?

You want to want to speak.
No is as irrelevant,
now, as *Yes* is.

And recall, startled,
how animal humanity
is: insistently walking
though femurs, vertebrae,
clavicles–and the smaller
bones: lunate, cuboid,
lachrymal–track earlier failures
scavenging each wayside
ahead, useless as all the years
sandpapered off this body.

There is ever more to do,
and there is so little of a person
once they've given.

*How will we know
if this migration
was useless?*

PEREGRINATIONS

How many rivers have we forded,
how much of the ocean do we bear upon us,
from protozoa to primates?

Intestines on the road this morning.

He is waiting for the beaver pond to flood
but it won't and he knows this. They dig.
A pine marten weasels at their packs
where a frog, innocently, seeks refuge.

Only ten more work-days before re-exodus
to the ocean. He will walk the tugboat quay
where a silkie surfaced, looked at him too full,
knowing the tempestuous world of the flood.

How do we atlas the ocean?

Bags are dragged and tilted
against shovel blades, sharp-tongued
and mute. The frog, at full tilt,
is ignored even when the marten
finds it with thinly teeth. Shakes twice.
Drags into her burrow.
　　Witness.
He finishes his sandwich
and work begets, begets again.

From protozoa to primate,
each rain teethes salt from our inner shoals.

Intestines on the road this evening, unmoved.

On the way home he muds a lodge
around his inner corpus. There may be no flood;
even so he is learning to hold his breath.

Can we ignore the brackish tide of our genes?

PRINCIPLE OF FAUNAL SUCCESSION

There's a non-compete clause in the low, laggard slats
of our feet, muscles pleated and smote
on stone, shovel, burnt or rotted deadfall.
The sweet, opened earth. The scents of the sun
are second-degree lesions. Our impurities slag us skin-thick;
how we wish a serpent had gifted our evolution with moult.
    Beneath this light there is no jurisprudence for touch.

Learn to eat before being the empty inner curds of aspen,
tunneled by ants. Every blueberry patch is more saviour
than deities, sacrifice, sweet grass and animal fat burnt
to honour the taboos we anchor 'round the pelvis we've shared
beyond three million years. Bigotries calcify
into bright coral reef; the living skies
ocean around our drowning.
    This culture teaches emptiness.

We scrawny 'til no fat tars our bodies
after the bushwhacking, the burning nerves
which puppet each skeleton;
we are only so malleable beneath the polities
our shovels inform –
    kicked 'til they break.

We hike back to the 'copter, rosehips and brambles in our knees.
The skies the rotor perforates are simply another collateral.
The sun's yoke will squat upon us two more weeks,
as if there isn't enough to bear in the thin,
raw caul that is our stubborn persistence.
   Today, my feet fracture like stones heated to boil water,
   a patternless angular breaking.
   I'll walk far as I may be able to eat the blueberries.

   There is no going back
      empty.

PRINCIPLE OF SUPERPOSITION

You migrate these fire-hardened trees –
spliced right through bark and phylum,
in great orange veins, to heartwood –
broken like the first shore,
suddenly dry above the flood.

> *The land is high here, sandy.*
> *You would have taken refuge*
> *here: a bed of needles,*
> *snow held above in the conifers.*

East of the Athabasca, the sun stretches
thinly flat against river. Throat, larynx, lungs
corrode in the smoke and each breath rips.
The burning forest is an imprint on your vision:
a body against you at night and the smell
of lilacs through the window
opened only for passage through night;
one arm laid against their breathing
while you remain awake.
    Their sound.
    Their smell.

Your 40 cm-by-40 cm descends 23 cm
where you revive the red mottled glacier gravel
moraine and this digging awakens
ancient fresh-water beach:
beaver tail-whack on water,
winter's cold percussion,
bison wallows darkly after rain.
There are so few animals, now, to witness.

Day smogs into moth hour
and smoke is thick as fog
on coast transects, your spine
burdened beneath the sun.

Fire floods across the river tonight,
like ocean hewn gritly across beach.

  From that vantage, you can almost imagine
  the glaciers, skies you could walk into.

Tomorrow, lilacs grow from ashes
cast adrift against the next first shore.

SURVIVAL

The waves are green, warmly. The spray, cool beneath the sun.
You lean into the wind, and this boat carries you where you please.

Storm resuscitates across horizon (because,
mustn't there always be fury?) and you run ahead,
fast as it throws itself into your canvas.

Against the rains and thunders, this world.
It demands to swallow you whole.
You traverse like pelican/albatross/pigeon.

What if your limbs shrank and finned, blood thinned,
skin scaled and you dove beneath? Not so far down
as your expectation, the water calms, darkly.

It is not you to squirm amongst the deeps
and wait and wait, and eat your lessers.

You take in and let out as a mythic beast stretches
sorcery/awe and a shadow cascading the cities,
and who follows your flight path;

each storm is nothing to what you may accomplish.

BLASTOCYST

For Fred and Nora

The bay kicks in bursts, salts our feet, slickens bedrock with darkness.
　　Ocean hauled across stone, drum-headed, a uterine sac –
　　a breaking held back. On the apostolic spur, a crab's foetid carcass:
　　gull-shucked and slack.
You peel back clothes and allow witness of your webbed

　　　　scars, rumpled but complete; a cowl of water
　　　　always gilled to your heart like a shield, a psalter.

What protects erodes, you say, *and self is more than ebb*
or zygote, which may or may not find purchase. From this we squirm,

　　　　I ask, *Into our own fast?* Ocean cleanses our feet, amniotic and cold.
　　You are not censored; evening spatters the kelp-haired berm.
　　　　Scudding mist comes in. Holds us wreck-by-fold.

　　　　Love, you say, *is to instrument a reckoning never allowed.*
　　The gaps between hands held; a consecration; but flawed.

LOVE, AT DISTANCE

You could discuss in the kestrel's tongue:
pacifying insects, amphibians,
and the smaller mammals in the muskeg.
You could whisper in the way partners
articulate love like *Panthera Onca*
through ferns in the forests of the night.
The rushes are thick like your incense hair,
(but rectitude is just privatization)
and morning hunts deep into our barrows.
You whisper, *Predation, ossuary,*
Leviticus, prey, abrogation.

I am chilled and callous when I wake.

REPARATION

I remember our lying in the dark, some slow divestment skinning
into morning, and thunderstorms on the horizons. Your hand

recorded on my breast some weak distress, signalling the tide
of our waking: slate-ghost waves lapping against the skin

that maps our borders, beckoning swimmers into the rip.
After drowning, this devastating tabloid: there is no glory –

and you fell me back into brutal slumber, as if to say:
   you may only leave
      – and none are allowed reparation.

DIGSITE

"These are our mountains... these are our stars."
—Carmen Aguirre, *Something Fierce*

The aspen are an ocean and the pines
spume against the crest of moraines
where glaciers bivalved their bellies
across dust and gravel.
Paid break is finished.

And you will fail to fall into step,
pace momentous from months lost
and the places you knew,
to which you may return, are sideways
and out-of-step. At the last call
you will dance but no one stands
together or looks into another's eyes,
and there is nothing left to belonging.

Blackflies tuber through layered clothes,
crawling your inner shirt, parasiting in under
the head net: in the loose folds
mossies land and inject long mouths
into ears, lips, scalp, and neck.
The blackflies stick into the corners
of your eyes like dull beasts in tar pits.

The dirt has delved so far under nails
it stains you the dark grey/browns of clay,
right to elbows, like a moist, secondary epidermis.
You're grateful and delirious for long sleeves
so the sun may not kiln you into pottery
and everywhere you melt off yourself;
stagnate; midges lay eggs in your waste.

Tonight, you wash old cuts and new ones
from the sharp, broken stones of the earth.
All angles, their blade thinness jammed
into the screen and you ran palms across
the stones without gloves so as to feel closely.
Those lithic fragments severed you open,
the sudden darkness of your body
lynx-pelting across the grey, mossed,
turned-away napes of the thinly aspen.

Morning to evening each day the sun
weighs upon you like a ritual
pyre. Like a warrior, when you die
you desire burning in salt or fire –
a literature conserved to the earth,
submerged elliptic currents
of river people once swam,
once drank from: a mythos raw cave-painted
from figures who may only renew when,
at last, returned to dirt. These are the waters
you may not drink, apostle or apostate;
this water taxed from atmosphere
after the heat has brought down storms.
The waters you may not drink leave your mouth coyly

sweet like coconut, needing something
more visceral, the uncertainty of a mouth
made certain; that smell missing
when you arise: an apiary
vivisected swarming the coulees.
When you die, should the sun devour you now,
the minerals which salt your atlas
flesh will be burnt away entire. Fire
will dissipate your facile body
back into language, the first shore.

But on the plane home all that matters is arrival.
The need to return to places you love –
the streets limited only by ocean taste
spray so unlike pine, aspen, muskeg;
and eat at diners where the staff still hasn't changed
as if there's nowhere to want to go,
nothing else more than service.

It's a single underwhelming repast.

There are no kestrels here, no hunting.
The movement of the ocean isn't time,
no metaphor for rejuvenation or endlessness,
just your feet estrangely chewing gritly beach
Metre-by-metre, living-by-living.
And how you desire, now, to sink
beneath the earth and find –
language, mythos, literature –
or just to find any lack therefore.

Muskeg floods boots at biblical capacity.
Sunk down to mid-thigh into moss and murk
but there's only 2 km left to swamp.
Wet now, may as well rough it.
Kestrels watch from willow and rush.
Kestrels hunting insects,
mammals, frogs. The kestrels sound
the empty in your heart.

And where is the warrior, you think.
Where the queen and the sacrificed lucky
to be strangled and thrown to the gods?
Literature like your skeleton, capitulated in mud,
flaccidly sunk. And who is the dull beast now?
You gaggle back sandy throat –
a raven there fettered in dust and burrs.
It reaches its beak from your mouth
and returns, knowing the hair of prey
you haven't yet scented; this language you call yours
dispossessed like following a firth
in the dark, to the inlet, to the soft fires
of meaning. What gist and denotation
the tongue so easily miscommits
need not be spoken.

And where is there one, you think, who enters
the bear's earth and is rejuvenated,
awakened from the furrow without
asking for favour or valediction?

But you cannot think, now, of treaty;
traversing windblown, bug-breathed cut-lines
which move always in-and-out of GPS
boundaries you're committed to stay within,
maybe a few metres off, and every water-crossing
is uncertain the way a mouth is uncertain:
never knowing how deep the waters speak.

You may one day enunciate this,
but you may not escape
the body always in twos; always
a body returned to the furrow.

The moment, a tide that eddies in cuts and churns;
seal surface above flood; raven gulps frog;
above shoreline – there are no apologetics for you, now,
because theodicy may not coexist
with any hunt but its own.

Your own extirpation forcefully within you,
living, even all things redacted to dirt;
could you learn timeless love without
time limit; the mythology of love?

You walk into rain, back into rent
and the meals you must reteach yourself
to cook; the anti-epiphany ends:

tonight your dreams are kestrels in willow cities,
and rushes and the long-tongued grasses.
Tonight you dream of places abandoned,
running the streets you revoked
in the darkness of your severed body,
waiting for the earth to rise beneath
you or prairie suddenly or mountain
trails that redact you into the slender
pelts of your ancestors. Running home,
cement furlongs furrow frail joints,
and the earth is silenced with streets paved
atop its mythos, and you may not drink
this water and you cannot remember your own firths
and stories, the old berths, and you cannot recall
the raven's language in your mouth.

Skyscrapers plummet the cities of kestrels,
and there is nowhere left to belong.

THE SILENT SPRUCE

Sawing down dead spruce for their tripods
he finds a steel trap for catching wolves, bears,
wolverines. If not for rust it would've broken
his ankle. The trap is the words that won't come –

a raven in his larynx, tarred and feathered,
brutish in fricatives and consonants.
He means to tell those little details,
grottos only he knows and means to take you
but he may only ant in frustration.

The forest has been scorched through,
the words that won't come mined out.
The land forbids what humble psychopomps
remain: kestrel, raven, frog. What muses are these?

The forest refuses this burnt dirt,
fire-hardened boles and bark, parting, crumbling
in rain. He digs it up. The forest keeps silent.

ACKNOWLEDGEMENTS

The following poems have been previously published in the following publications: "Reparation" in *The Scores*; "HhOw 53" and "Hunter" in *Prairie Fire*; "Manitoba Solstice" in *Poems from Planet Earth* (Leaf Press, 2013).

ABOUT THE AUTHOR

Owain Nicholson grew up in Winnipeg and studied both creative writing and archaeology at the University of Victoria. A working archaeologist, Nicholson sees history, ancestry, nature and people at the centre of both practices, and his poems often use the digsite as a source of image and metaphor. Nicholson currently lives and works in Alberta and BC, and studies in Ontario.

PHOTO CREDIT: MIA WATKINS